The Ghosts of Izieu

JAMES WATSON

Level 3

Retold by John Escott

Series Editors: Andy Hopkins and Jocelyn Potter

Pearson Education Limited
Edinburgh Gate, Harlow,
Essex CM20 2JE, England
and Associated Companies throughout the world.

ISBN 0 582 42654 5

First published 2000

Typeset by Digital Type, London
Set in 11/14pt Bembo
Printed in Spain by Mateu Cromo, S. A. Pinto (Madrid)

Published by Pearson Education Limited in association with
Penguin Books Ltd, both companies being subsidiaries of Pearson Plc

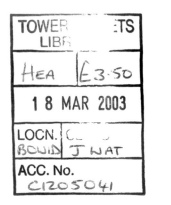
For a complete list of the titles available in the Penguin Readers series please write to your local
Pearson Education office or to: Marketing Department, Penguin Longman Publishing,
80 Strand, London, WC2R 0RL

Contents

Dedication

For my wife, Kitty, who died 5 August 1998;
with thanks for her love, her companionship and her support.

Introduction

Grey light came from between the bedroom curtains, like the light of an old black and white film. In it she could see boys and girls in coats. They were carrying packages, and some had bags over their shoulders.

Who are these children? Where are they going? Are they real, or is Elise seeing ghosts from the past? And why did her father bring her to this little French village? What secrets does it hide?

When Elise finds herself in another time, some of the answers become clear. She learns some of the terrible facts of war. And she discovers who the children are.

James Watson is a very successful writer. He has written plays for radio, but most of his books are for younger people. This story was written specially for Penguin Readers.

Other books by James Watson are *Sign of the Swallow* (1967), *The Bull Leapers* (1970), *Legion of the White Tiger* (1973), *The Freedom Tree* (1976), *Talking in Whispers* (1983), *Where Nobody Sees* (1987), *Make Your Move, and Other Stories* (1988), *No Surrender* (1991), *Ticket to Prague* (1993) and *Justice of the Dagger* (1998).

James Watson has three daughters and two granddaughters. He enjoys swimming and the successes of Blackburn Rovers football team.

Chapter 1 The Ghost Children

'She didn't want to come, Steve,' said Carol. 'And now she says that she can see ghosts.' She looked out of the window on to the war memorial in the village square. Everything was silent. Her new husband called it 'a dusty French silence'. Carol called it a dusty *hot* French silence. It was only April, but it was almost too hot to move.

'I've tried very hard,' Carol continued. 'But she refuses to be my friend.'

'Ghosts?' asked Steve. He was here to rest after a heart attack. Already he was tired of healthy food, no long walks, no heavy drinking and no smoking. 'What sort of ghosts?'

'Oh, I didn't ask,' said Carol. 'Ghosts are ghosts.'

'We'll just have to be patient with her,' replied Steve.

'But it's three years since her mother left you.'

Steve answered her with a sad smile. 'Perhaps Elise isn't happy with you. But that doesn't mean that she's happy with her Mum. Things will get better.'

'You always say that,' said Carol. 'The girl hates me.'

'She's sixteen, Carol,' Steve said. 'She's unhappy. You're new in our lives, and she's not sure about you.'

'When I look at her, she jumps,' said Carol. 'When I come into the room, she leaves it.'

It was very nice to be in love, Carol decided. But it was different being married and a stepmother. She picked up her bag of drawing and painting things. 'I'm going out to paint.'

Steve smiled at her. 'Don't get too friendly with any ghosts!' He tried to put his arm round her, but she pushed him away.

'Didn't I do that when I joined this family?' she said.

♦

1

Elise woke up – and there again was the same image, in the same place. It was exactly the same as yesterday morning.

'It's the light,' she thought. Grey light came from between the bedroom curtains, like the light of an old black and white film. In it she could see boys and girls in coats. They were carrying packages, and some had bags over their shoulders. And was that an army lorry?

She watched for a minute. Then she got up to look out. The village square was empty except for a few cars. Some birds flew above the war memorial in the early morning sun.

'I can't explain it scientifically,' she thought. 'But I'm guessing that the village square gets mirrored in the room. It's as simple as that. And the lorry? Well that's the "school bus" in this little village. But why didn't I see the lorry drive away? Why didn't I hear it?'

She stood at the window. The birds were on the war memorial now, and on the ground in front of it. Could the *birds* be the schoolchildren?

Elise began to get dressed. 'So that's my excitement for the day,' she thought. 'This is going to be my most boring holiday ever!'

She looked across at the village church.

'Dad says that there are some wonderful coloured windows in the church,' she thought. 'Thanks, Dad! And after I see those, I can read some gravestones! Or there's the wooden Mother and Child. Dad says I can take photos of it. And Carol can do a drawing. Well, Carol and I agree on one thing: Dad's idea of an exciting holiday is worse than two hours of homework!'

Elise could not get the image of the lorry and the children out of her mind. The lorry was green and dark brown. 'Was it an army vehicle?' she thought suddenly.

The door below went BANG! as it closed. Elise watched Carol escape with her painting things. 'Is she angry with Dad

They were carrying packages, and some had bags over their shoulders.

already?' she thought. 'Poor Carol. I don't make things easy for her, but she still tries hard. I'm in the way, I realize that. She wants Dad for herself. And she isn't happy when I talk about ghosts. She's a very sensible person, and sensible people don't believe in ghosts. She thinks it's all in my head. I told her about the children – twenty or thirty of them – but she just shook her head. "So many children in this small village? I don't think so," she said. "Why don't we see them at other times of the day?" "Because they're ghosts." But she doesn't believe in ghosts. "You're the only person who sees them," she said. She talks to me the way that my real Mum does. And she's *not* my real Mum!'

Elise went downstairs.

Chapter 2   Stefan

She was glad to talk to her father alone.

'Dad, I think I saw some ghosts,' she said.

'Yes, your Mother – sorry – Carol told me,' he replied.

'She doesn't like me to talk about them.'

'I don't want you to worry about it,' he said. 'Just enjoy your holiday.'

'I'm not worried,' said Elise. 'I'm just interested.'

'We'll have a drive out in the car this afternoon,' he suggested. 'There are lots of things to see. Would you like that?'

'Would I like that? I'm not six years old, Dad!' said Elise. 'Oh, why did we come here?'

'We often stayed in houses in France with your Mum.'

Elise thought about saying, 'Perhaps she left you because our lives were too boring.' But she decided not to make two enemies in one day.

'Why do you always visit those war graves?' she asked.

'I like history,' her father said. 'You know that.'

'But why graves?'

'Not graves, exactly – memorials,' he explained. 'For me, they're like doors into the past.'

'But always wars – people who died.'

'They're people who gave their lives for us,' said her father. 'We mustn't forget that.'

'Are there any war graves near here, Dad?' she asked.

'Not graves, no.'

'Then why are we here?'

'So I can get better – doctor's orders,' he said.

'You've brought your notebooks, Dad. Why?'

'Maybe I'll need them,' he said.

'What for?' she said.

Elise's father put his finger to his mouth. 'Doctor's orders!'

She left him to rest. 'Doctor's orders?' she thought. 'I don't think so. He's got a secret.'

◆

The boy on the church steps was local. When Elise, Carol and her Dad arrived in the village, he was with a group of other boys around the war memorial. He waved, while another boy shouted something about Manchester United.

Was he waiting for her now? He seemed very nervous as she got near the church entrance.

'*Bonjour!*'★ she said.

Did girls in France just introduce themselves to boys? Elise was not sure. But she needed to talk to *somebody* her own age during these two weeks in the middle of nowhere.

'And of course I need to practise my French,' she thought.

The boy turned away, but he fell.

★ *Bonjour; merci; pardonnez-mois; Je suis anglaise; au revoir.* French words for *hello; thank you; sorry; I'm English; goodbye.*

'I work at the farm. At Lolinoz,' he said.

Elise said, in English, 'Are you all right?' She even offered him a hand.

The boy looked at her and accepted the hand. He was small, but quite good-looking. '*Merci*,' he said. 'You German?'

'No, me English.' The words just came out like that and Elise went bright red in the face. '*Pardonnez-moi. Je suis anglaise.*'

In French, the boy said, 'I must go. I have to get back. Thank you, yes. You are very kind. The English, I like. And the Russians, even. Italians – great!'

'Germans?' asked Elise quickly.

'I work at the farm. At Lolinoz,' he said.

'Is that far?' she asked.

'No,' he said. 'It's just up the road.'

'What do you do on the farm?' she asked.

'Everything,' he said. 'But I must go.'

He seemed a very lonely boy. She almost said to him, 'Don't look so worried. Nobody's going to hurt you.' But how could she be sure of that?

'It's lovely round here,' she said.

'Yes.' He was in a hurry to go, but he was polite. Two or three times he looked over his shoulder.

'All these little country roads,' she said in English. 'My Dad got lost four or five times before we found the village. It's so ... lonely.'

'Yes ... hidden,' the boy said.

Was he talking of secrets?

'Mysterious?' she suggested.

'Yes,' he said.

'What's your name?' she asked. 'Mine's Elise.'

'Stefan,' he said.

'That's strange,' she said. 'My Dad's called Stephen. With a "ph". But everybody calls him Steve with a "v".'

He smiled. 'Your mother, she is the painter?'

'She's not exactly my mother,' Elise said. 'My Dad married again. Do you have the same parents that you started with?' Elise was pleased with that sentence. Her French was getting better.

Stefan shook his head. He lived with his uncle and aunt on the farm.

Elise nearly replied, 'Parents aren't always so wonderful.' But she stopped herself. You can't be rude about parents to somebody who hasn't got any. So she asked, 'Is it a big farm?'

Again, a shake of the head.

'Animals?' she said.

'Fifteen,' he said. 'And we make wine. Very good wine.'

'Perhaps I can come and watch,' Elise suggested.

His nervousness returned. He looked over Elise's shoulder across the village square. She followed his eyes.

He was watching the entrance of the town hall, a beautiful building.

'Do you know someone in there, Stefan?' she asked. 'Perhaps you can show me the inside one day.'

'I have to go,' Stefan said.

'I can help you with your English and –'

'Pardon – I must go,' he repeated.

'Are you in trouble?' asked Elise.

'Trouble?'

'With your uncle?' she said. 'With the police?'

'Police?' he said quickly. He looked afraid.

It was a mistake. She was frightening him, when she only wanted to be his friend. He stepped out of the long shadow of the church.

'Please don't hurry away,' she said. 'I'm always asking people stupid questions. It gets *me* into trouble.'

He answered with a smile – a lovely smile.

'You're nice,' he said. 'Thank you. Your French is very good.' Stefan held out his hand. '*Au revoir!*'

'Perhaps I'll see you another time,' she said. 'I'm here for two weeks.'

'Perhaps,' he replied. 'Goodbye!'

Chapter 3   Back in Time

She watched him as he walked across the village square. He stopped and looked round. And then he ran.

'Lolinoz. I must remember the name,' she thought. She imagined a dusty brown farmhouse in the hills.

But why did he hurry away like that? Elise looked round. What frightened him? 'There's something strange about this place,' she thought. 'Carol noticed it too. She feels uncomfortable here – it's so quiet.'

Elise looked at the church. She thought about the stories that it could tell. It was hundreds of years old. What did it see in that time? She couldn't think of anything to do, so she opened the church door.

It was colder inside and, yes – mysterious. At the east end were three round windows. The coloured glass of the centre window was very bright. It hurt her eyes to look at it. Her father was right. It was a beautiful window. Of course, he could stand and look at it for hours.

Elise sat down on one of the seats at the front and looked around her at the pictures and the flowers. She imagined ghosts. 'Come and haunt me,' she said, and she spoke the words. 'If you don't, I'll die. This place is so boring. No? OK, *don't* then.'

She thought about Stefan. Was he a friend? 'He's a strange boy, but he's got a thoughtful face. For a minute or two he was very friendly. Then ... I don't know. Why are boys afraid of girls?'

Elise got up and walked towards a side-room. Against the far wall was the wooden Mother and Child. She stood in front of it. She said softly, '*You* didn't leave your child for another man.' And then, more loudly, '*Why* can't I be angry with them? They've destroyed my life. Dad, Mum and now Carol. I'm so unhappy!'

She closed her eyes. She could smell the flowers. Suddenly, she thought, 'This is silly. It won't help if I'm difficult with people.' She opened her eyes and looked at the beautiful spring flowers. She felt better, but tears began to run down her face.

She thought: 'I can tell Carol about the flowers. Or will she just say, "I don't paint flowers"?'

She suddenly felt cold. Even on a hot day these old churches were as cold as the grave.

Elise walked towards the north door. She was shaking. 'It isn't really very cold,' she told herself. She stopped at a table near the heavy wooden door. She decided to sign her name in the Visitors' Book.

She opened the book. 'That's strange,' she thought. 'Nobody's put their name in since – 1944!'

Was it a joke? She turned back a page. No, there weren't any signatures after 1944, but there were plenty before that. There were notes about the beautiful windows, and about the Mother and Child. One was dated 1939 – the year that the Second World War began. It asked for God's protection. It ended: *God help us!*

'Dad will be interested in this,' Elise thought. 'He'll spend the rest of the holiday studying it. Perhaps that's why he brought his notebooks.'

She looked again at the last note, and the name after it. She could not read the surname. But when she saw the first name, her eyes opened wide with surprise.

The name in the Visitors' Book was similar to hers, but not the same: *Eloise*.

'I think I'll get out into the sunlight,' decided Elise.

She remembered the other words: *God help us!*

Elise decided not to add her signature to the Visitors' Book. Or not now. 'Maybe if Dad comes with me,' she thought.

The silence of the church was broken by a woman's voice: 'Eloise! You must come now.'

Elise did not hear the north door open . . .

♦

. . . but the door is open now. A woman with straight grey hair is looking at her. 'You must not walk in the village, Eloise. It is not safe,' the woman is saying.

Elise moves towards the woman. She can't stop herself. 'I am not Eloise – Elise is my name.' These words are in her head but she can't say them. The light is bad in the church. The woman has made a mistake.

The woman puts a hand on her arm. 'Why do you do these things – and risk everything?'

'Risk? Everything?'

'You must remember the rules, Eloise.'

They are going down the church steps into the street. Everything looks different from here. You can't even see the war memorial.

Elise tries to pull away from the woman. 'I think I shall be all right now,' she says. She tries to be polite. In the sunlight the woman will realize her mistake.

'You like to do what you want, my child, but –'

'Yes, I do,' says Elise. 'Now, please leave me –'

'I can't leave you here. We will *all* die.'

Elise does not know the road that they are taking out of the village. The woman's hand holds tightly to Elise's arm. She is taller than Elise and stronger.

'Excuse me.' Elise tries to stop, but the woman pulls her along the road.

'To Lolinoz — now!'

Elise remembers the name. 'The farm?' she says.

'Of course, child,' says the woman.

'Where Stefan lives?' asks Elise.

'Where we all live, Eloise,' says the woman. 'I sometimes think you are stupid.'

How does she know my name? Or almost my name.

There are white rocks between the trees above them, and large black birds on the rocks and in the trees.

'It's all right,' Elise says, pulling her arm away from the woman. She smiles. 'I'll come quietly.'

'Won't Stefan be surprised?' she thinks.

The road is narrow. Soon the spring plants will grow and hide these rock faces.

Suddenly the woman pushes Elise off the road and into the trees. The sound of a car comes from the road in front of them.

'Don't move!' says the woman.

'But —'

'Don't move!'

It is an old car, from years ago. It passes. The woman waits, but does not explain. Then she takes Elise back on to the road.

She says, 'Now you understand?'

Elise does not understand. She is frightened.

Elise remembers stories from the newspapers — stories of tourists murdered in the lonely French countryside. A woman who went out on a bicycle, for example, and was never seen again.

She remembers her father's words: 'Stay close to the village centre. Always tell us where you're going.'

'Lolinoz, Dad! Can you hear me?'

Suddenly the woman pushes Elise off the road and into the trees.

Stay calm. 'I'm afraid I can't stay long. I have to get back for lunch,' she says to the woman.

The woman is not listening. They are coming to some farm buildings. The farmhouse is off the road, and is built of the same stone as the church. They do not take the main path to the front of the farmhouse.

Trees hide the road. 'You've got animals, I think,' says Elise. 'I like animals.' Her voice tells her that she is nervous.

Suddenly, a high, windowless wall hides the sun. It is cold in the shadows. 'Where are we going?' she asks.

No answer; but the strong hand is back on Elise's arm. She is walking past a door in the wall but is pulled back. The woman takes out a large key.

'In, child,' she says.

'I really think – ' begins Elise.

The door opens on to a dark room and wooden stairs. There is an old smell of animals. The woman locks the door from the inside.

Elise moves back against the wall. 'I really must ask you to explain,' she says.

The woman does not answer. She pushes Elise up the stairs, but this time the touch is more friendly; and there is almost a smile on the woman's face. 'Eloise, will you never accept the facts?' asks the woman.

'Where are you taking me?' Elise says. 'I want to know. You've made a mistake. My name isn't Eloise.'

'You're making me angry, girl,' answers the woman.

'Really?' says Elise. 'Well I'm glad. Until you tell me –'

The woman lifts her hand. She is going to hit Elise across the face, but stops at the last second. The speed of it, the danger of it, frightens Elise.

'Why fight?' she thinks. 'I'll find out what's happening soon.'

14

Chapter 4   The Children

The stairs are long, and at the top the walls open into a roof space. Sunlight from windows opposite the stairs leave everything in darkness.

'Now,' says the woman, 'you will explain to Sabina.'

'I'm not sure what –' Elise stops. Now she can see the rest of the room.

It is large, half in shadow, the top floor of a farm building. There are children, thirty of them or perhaps more than thirty. Some are playing quietly; some are reading; some are sleeping – but already there is a crowd of them in front of Elise.

'Eloise has come back!'

'They know me too,' thinks Elise. She says, 'Stefan?'

The younger children move away. A boy comes towards her.

'But this isn't Stefan!' she decides.

Now Elise is safely inside, the woman is not angry. She speaks like a mother. 'He is *our* Stefan,' she says.

This boy is younger, with darker skin. Good-looking, but not *Elise's* Stefan.

She holds out her hand. It is the polite thing in France when you are introduced for the first time to a stranger. But Stefan does not take it.

He says, 'Sabina is angry with you. But we have all asked her to be kind to you.' He smiles – a smile to someone that he has loved all his life.

Someone has called Sabina. She walks with her head high in the air. She is clearly the boss in this place. Her hair is pulled tightly back from her face. She has a proud nose, and eyes that read you in a minute.

'Well, why did you go this time, Eloise?' she asks. But she is not interested in the answer. 'You have too much trust in the good people of this village. I have told you that before. You think

He is angry with her, and not ready to forgive.

that they have taken us to their hearts. And, yes, we are not a secret now.

'But they are afraid. And sometimes fear is too much for people. How many times do I have to explain that to you? Every day the villagers are taking more risks.

'When you go off alone like that, you put *them* in danger – not just us. When one person's fear becomes too strong, we are finished. One person. One letter. One short phone call.'

Elise doesn't understand. She too is afraid. The children are so silent, she realizes suddenly. When they speak, they speak very softly. All these children in one place, but the place is as quiet as a church.

Elise is asked to sit down with the rest. She is cold with worry. She repeats to herself, slowly, 'I've never seen these people, but they know me. And I *know* I'm not dreaming.'

Stefan sits next to her on the wooden floor. She tries a smile.

'It is not funny, Eloise,' he says.

She waits. He is angry with her, and not ready to forgive. 'Is this a school?' she asks. 'Are you hiding?'

Stefan does not seem to think that this is funny either. He tries to think of an answer. But before he can put thoughts into words, Sabina stands in front of the children.

'You have all been good,' she says. 'Very good. Except Eloise. Many of you have asked, "Isn't the village safe? They are helping to hide us, so why can't we go out and play?"

'In your hearts, you know the answer. The risk is too great. People know that we are here, yes. But it is also a secret. They do not see us, so they try not to think about us.'

Elise looks round at the children. The word in her head is – refugees. They are dressed in other people's clothes; most of them are too big or too tight. And they look ready to pick up their things and leave at any minute.

'One thing's sure,' she thinks. 'This isn't happening *now*, in my time.' In her mind she remembers her steps to the church. The sudden cold in the air. And the last signature in the Visitors' Book, dated 1944.

Not a joke.

Elise remembers her morning image of children climbing on to a lorry in the village square. Was that in 1944? She is sure now that it was.

Sabina speaks again. Elise is right. 'The Gestapo★ have visited Belley,' Sabina says. 'That is a small market town very close to us. The Gestapo chiefs at Lyons want very much to find people like us. You know this.' She stops. She does not want to frighten the children. 'They would like to ask us questions.

'The countryside is too large to search completely. That is why you are here. We call it Izieu the Hidden. But Belley! That is too near here!

'In other villages, they are stopping people in the street and asking questions. And knocking on doors. God will protect us. He has until now. But we must be very, very careful.'

Sabina smiles. 'We have been here for ten months. Perhaps one day soon the war will end. The Germans will leave France for ever. People in town say that American and British soldiers aren't far away. So there's hope, you see.

'Tomorrow, I shall look for new hiding places for us. But I am afraid that you won't all be able to stay together.'

A cry goes up from the children. Stefan looks quickly at Elise, then says to Sabina, 'We are all friends!'

'We want to stay together!' says a voice from the back of the group.

Another asks, 'Did the Gestapo take our mums and dads away?'

★ Gestapo: Germany's secret police in the Second World War (1939–45).

The same thought fills the heart of every child there. Elise remembers her history lessons – and she is filled with fear.

The Gestapo! The worst of Hitler's men. The men who sent thousands of Jews in lorries to the concentration camps.

To Auschwitz . . .

To Belsen . . .

To Buchenwald . . .

To Dachau . . .

To Treblinka . . .

She knows them all. The sound of their names fills her with fear. She knows from Dad of the terrible things that happened in those places. 'It's right to know about these things,' he believed. 'We *must* remember.'

◆

One image stayed in Elise's head for a long time after she saw it in a book. A photograph of a mountain of shoes.

'Where do you think the owners of those shoes went?' Dad asked her. 'What do you think happened to them?'

'Dead?' she said.

'Dead! And how do you think all those people died?'

She did not want to know. But she knew that he wanted to tell her.

But he did not. He kept his feelings to himself. 'There are a lot of people who do not want to remember these things,' he said. 'They prefer to forget history.'

'But not you,' thought Elise. 'You want to continue fighting for those dead people. But does it really help?'

When they arrived in this strange village, Elise said, 'Dad, why did you bring us to this place?'

And he answered, 'There is a secret here.'

Carol was also nervous about Dad's interest. 'You think too much about the past, Stephen,' she said.

Elise did not listen to Dad's reply. At that time – but not now – she agreed with Carol's feelings. It was unhealthy to think too much about the past.

♦

Now she remembers Dad's answer: 'I think I have a different idea of time to other people.' Elise is living now through things that happened to people in history. Terrible things. Too terrible to think about, even for people who are safe and far away.

For Elise the past has become her future. 'Come and save me, Dad – please!' she thinks.

Sabina finishes speaking. 'I've told our helpers, "When I'm away, keep your eyes and ears open!" You remember the story that I told you? The story about Cerberus, the watchdog who never sleeps?'

'He had three heads,' says one of the children.

'Yes, and when he was on guard, one of his heads never, ever slept.'

The children smile. They repeat after Sabina: 'Never, ever slept!'

'And we must be as careful as the eyes of Cerberus.'

Sabina has turned to Elise. 'I want you to promise something, Eloise,' she says. 'Promise that you will never, ever go off alone again.'

Elise is suddenly tired, not just afraid. But she says, 'And if I don't?'

'All our lives will be at risk – you know that,' says Sabina.

Stefan is standing near them, and some of the children are listening. It seems to be important to them that she listens to Sabina. Elise understands that she must be sensible now. She must be an example to the other children. But if she promises not to go off alone again, she will risk *her* life. How can she escape?

She speaks her next words carefully.

'All right. Eloise –' She stops. Then she repeats that other name. 'Eloise promises not to go off alone again. She promises not to escape.'

For a second, the word 'escape' worries Sabina. That is not the word that she used. It is not what she was thinking about. She is going to speak when Stefan says, 'I'll be Eloise's special Cerberus. Don't worry.'

Elise is not pleased by this. 'I don't need a spy to help me keep my promises,' she says.

She has hurt him. He moves away, but Sabina is thinking about other things. As she goes out, she calls softly to all the children, 'Remember Cerberus!'

Chapter 5 A Terrible Mistake

Elise finds a dark corner and looks down from the window. Below is a yard. She can just see the corner of the building opposite. Between the farmhouse and another building she can see trees climbing steeply to walls of rock.

'That's my path back to real life,' she thinks. 'If I stay here, perhaps I'll begin to forget my real life. I must tell myself – *I am not here*. This is not my time. How can it be?'

Elise is not left to her own thoughts. Stefan comes and sits next to her.

'Sorry about that,' he begins. 'I mean –'

She is not really angry with him. 'Nobody likes it when they are called a spy.'

'I didn't –'

'But that's what you meant.' She speaks more kindly. 'Isn't it?'

He shakes his head. Clearly there is something special between them. Between Stefan and Eloise. He watches her. He is younger. But he seems to think that he is wiser.

'You will not find your parents like that, Eloise. It doesn't help to run away.'

'I wasn't running away. And my parents are perfectly all right, thank you.'

'So you really believe what Sabina tells us all?' he says. Elise is silent. 'We older ones *know*.'

'Know?' She thinks, 'I am so afraid. I can't get away from here. Sabina has locked the downstairs door.' She says, 'Eloise is not my name. And also – '

She stops. The words will sound so silly.

'We will probably never see our parents again,' continues Stefan. 'We have been lucky here. But Belley! That is close.'

Elise turns away. There are tears in her eyes. For herself, yes. But also for Stefan and the children.

'So what do we not tell the younger children?' she hears herself ask, but she knows the answer.

'About the arrests,' says Stefan.

Elise thinks: 'Does Stefan really know?' But she says, 'My parents haven't been arrested. I'm sure of it.' She is surprised at herself. Is this Elise talking, or Eloise?

'That is what you always say,' replies Stefan. 'I understand. We all have our ways – '

'What do you mean?'

'We all have to live with this.'

'So what's your way?'

Stefan does not answer immediately. He is too calm for Elise. 'What do you think is going to happen to you, Stefan?' she asks.

He looks at her strangely. 'Why do you say "you"?' he says. 'If something happens to me, to us, it will happen to you too, Eloise.'

She is tired. She is frightened. Without thinking, she says angrily, 'Oh no, it won't. It won't. It can't. It's not possible. All this can't happen.'

He does not understand. 'Yes, it's difficult,' he says.

'No, not difficult! *It's not possible!*'

Stefan does not look surprised when she is angry and unpleasant. Perhaps Eloise is like that. But *Elise* does not want to be like that.

She notices that outside it is beginning to get dark. She looks at Stefan. 'He's the only person who can help me,' she decides. But if she tells him the true story, he will not believe her. How can he? She does not want to believe *his* true story. She smells dust. This is a different world. Not the world of Dad's rest after his heart attack. Or of Carol's oil paints. Not the world of computers and TVs. This is a world where death is everywhere.

Now Elise feels the terrible fear that Stefan feels. The fear that the women feel, and the children. But it's worse for her because she *knows*. She knows some of the terrible things that are going to happen. The women and children do not.

She can look back on all this from the future.

She thinks about the danger that she is in. Suddenly there is not enough air. She starts coughing. This is real fear. Stefan moves closer to her. He thinks he understands. He takes her hand in his hand, and his touch is a help to her.

She needs his help to save herself. They are both on their knees now, face to face. It feels good. She begins to speak slowly. 'Stefan . . . there are things that I can't explain. But I want you to help me to get away from here.'

His face, now in shadow, shows that he does not understand. 'Alone?' he asks.

'Yes, alone,' says Elise. 'I'm a danger to you all, you know that,' she says. 'Sabina was right.'

He seems very surprised. 'And the rest of us?' He shakes his head. 'No, we are all in this war *together.*'

The words come out before she can stop herself: 'They won't want me.'

'Not want you?' he says. 'What do you mean?'

He takes her hand in his hand, and his touch is a help to her.

'They won't want to take me,' she replies.

'The Gestapo?' Stefan laughs. 'You think they won't take you? Because you are pretty?'

'No, they won't want me!'

Too loud. Can other people hear?

'Why are you so special suddenly?' he says.

She shouts: 'If you must know – because I'm not a Jew!' The silence is full of ears. All eyes are turned on her. She feels she is falling . . . down . . .down . . .'I have said the worst thing,' she thinks.

Stefan asks, 'So why have you hidden with us all this time? Is your mother black? Are there crazy people in your family? You are here for a reason.'

'It's a mistake,' she tells him. 'A terrible mistake.'

'We are all mistakes, Eloise,' he says. 'Because we are Jews. That is why our dads and mums had to wear yellow stars on their coats. *You* told us about that, Eloise. And you talked about *us*. You were one of us. And when you are one of us, you can't just *stop* being one of us. They come –'

'Yes!' she shouts, angrily and without thinking. 'Yes! They come after you. They catch you and put you on trains. They take you to the concentration camps. I know, I know!'

She stops at the sound of her terrible words. 'I said the worst thing; but then I didn't stop,' she thinks.

One of the younger children asks, 'What trains?'

Elise is silent. In front of the others, will Stefan ask the worst question? The question about the worst thing? But the word goes round about trains.

'What trains?'

'We are going on a train?'

'Where to?'

'I love trains.'

'Will it be safe?'

'What does Madame Sabina say?'

Elise feels Stefan's eyes on her. It is the other question that he is asking in his silence. She wants to get away from him – from them. 'It's just something that I heard,' she says.

'Who from?'

'I forget.'

'Who told you about the trains?'

A child asks, 'Will they take all of us?'

'My mother and I counted the trains that went past our house,' says another child.

Stefan tries to turn the thoughts of the younger ones away from journeys to strange places. 'We are safe here,' he says. 'If we stay very quiet, there will be no trains.'

He is thinking like an adult, but the others act like children.

'Why can't we go on a train?'

'It's boring here all the time.'

A child *becomes* a train. It is the child who likes trains. She moves her arms and makes the right noises. 'Choo-choo-choo!' She goes slowly at first, then faster. The other children follow her. They put their hands round the waist of the child in front until the 'train' is halfway down the room.

'Where shall we go?'

'Marseilles!'

'Choo-choo-choo!'

'London!'

'Choo-choo-choo!'

'New York!'

'To the seaside!'

'To the mountains!'

The train of children moves happily round the room. It stops sometimes to pick up more passengers. Elise is left alone with Stefan.

'What do you know?' he asks her. 'Did someone tell you something in the village today?'

They put their hands round the waist of the child in front until the 'train' is halfway down the room.

'I spoke to no one,' she says.

'But you know something,' he says.

Elise shakes her head. 'I've no idea what happened to you!' she says. She is talking about *history* now. It happened before she was born.

Stefan does not understand her. 'We have all talked about what happened to us,' he says.

'No, I mean – ' Elise stops.

Now Stefan asks, 'Concentration camps? What are they?'

Elise thinks quickly. What story can she tell him? 'But he'll look into my eyes and he'll know,' she thinks. 'He'll ask questions until he knows.'

'I feel sick,' she says. 'Have you got some water?'

Stefan crosses the room to a table near the stairs. He returns with a bottle of water. He pours the water into a glass and looks at Elise. He is trying to understand her.

'He's a clever boy, but how can he understand me?' she thinks. She drinks the water.

'*Merci*,' she says. 'You're kind. And I'm sorry I said those things.'

'Then rest,' he says. They are friends again. He kisses her. 'Perhaps tomorrow the English will come, or the Americans. What do you think?'

'They'll come,' she replies softly, and she thinks: 'But will they be too late?'

Chapter 6   Escape from the Past

The sun has dropped behind the trees and rocks above the farm. The room is dark now. Elise lies in the darkness, but her eyes are open. The farm is not far from Izieu. She can hear the church clock as it sounds three. She looks at the sleeping children. Forty-four of them, safe, but never safe.

The pictures in her head are keeping her awake; pictures that she has seen in Dad's books. She can hear Dad's voice: 'Some trains went from Compiègne. We stayed there three years ago, remember? When things were all right with your Mum. From Compiègne they were taken to the camp at Dachau. Hundreds of them were dead when they arrived.'

'Why?'

'Illness, no food – they were pushed in together like animals. No, *worse* than animals!'

Dad got very angry when he talked of these things. 'How many days can you live without sitting down? Without a toilet? And, worst of all, without any water?'

Elise remembered the French children from pictures in Dad's book. They wore prison clothes, and their heads were shaved. It did not matter if they were old or young, male or female, healthy or sick. They were shown no kindness.

'The Nazis called it the "final solution",' said Dad.

'Was no one kind?' Elise asked her father when she saw the pictures. 'Not one person?'

'Oh yes, a few,' he said. 'Like Schindler. Remember the film? But never enough people.'

◆

'I must get out,' Elise thinks now. 'Dad, help me!' Suddenly she thinks, 'Did all this happen because of him?'

◆

She remembers times when Mum was angry with him: 'I'm tired of following you around war graves and concentration camps. It's not healthy!'

Her mother's final solution was simple. She walked out and left them. But it wasn't a solution, was it? Not for Elise, or for her father.

Elise remembered her father's answer. 'Not healthy? Can't we remember the millions who died? Can't we fight for a better world? Must we forget?'

'I never said that,' Elise's mother told him. 'But we can fight for a better world without crying in front of war memorials.'

'That's not all that I do. I protest – I go on marches –'

'And who did that help? You were arrested.'

'You protested too!'

◆

Elise thinks about Eloise. In her thoughts, she asks Eloise, 'Did you have the same problem with your parents?' She also has silent words for Dad: '*You* should be here now, not me.'

But she has a plan. A dangerous one for everybody, perhaps, but she has to do it.

During the afternoon, Elise has seen that the farm is built into the hillside. The ground outside climbs up steeply from right to left.

This end of the building opens on to the shortest drop from a window. It is time now for her final solution – her only solution. Go! Go, now! Don't wait. This is you, and this is also Eloise. Remember? Eloise likes to go off alone.

But can Eloise really leave her friends? 'I'm not Eloise!'

No one can help her now. She is not part of this history. But she must act now, or she will be lost in this time for ever. There will be Eloise, but no Elise.

Go!

Elise passes between the children. She stops at the end window. Pale moonlight comes through, and she looks at herself in the glass. 'I thought that ghosts could not see themselves in mirrors,' she thinks. 'That proves I'm not a ghost.'

The window is too cold and too hard; this cannot be a dream.

It is difficult to open. She hurts her hand trying. Will it open? Has it ever opened?

Elise looks behind her. Is one of the children watching her? Perhaps Stefan. 'I can say that I need air. It's so hot in here,' she thinks.

At last the window moves! But the noise! She looks at the children, but no one moves. She can just see their faces in the darkness. They will be in her memory for ever, like Dad's pictures of the concentration camps.

But perhaps it will all end differently – a story with a happy ending. Perhaps British or American soldiers will stop the lorries as they move through France. Who will ever know?

For a full minute, Elise waits. She cannot move – her feelings of pity for these new friends are too great. And there is also in her heart a sudden love for them.

Does Eloise love Stefan? Does Elise?

She remembers that morning's image in the town square of Izieu. The image of the children climbing into an army lorry. She understands now. Sabina is working so hard to hide the children. But she will fail. By accident or on purpose, someone has told the Gestapo about their hiding place.

Elise pushes the window open. 'When I've gone, the children won't remember me,' she tells herself. 'I don't exist in their time – not on 5 April 1944.'

She cannot see the ground. She won't be able to see it until she is almost out of the window. She won't be able to change her mind – to go back.

She jumps . . . she is falling. The ground is far below her.

Elise hits the ground. She hears the CRACK! of her foot before the pain from her fall shoots up her leg. She wants to scream with the pain. And more pain is coming from her chest.

'You can't scream,' she tells herself. 'You'll wake the children in

Elise puts her hand into her mouth.

the house. They'll call Sabina and she'll lock me in. Stefan will look at me and say, "How could you go and leave us?"'

So Elise puts her hand into her mouth. She tastes blood. The voice that said *Go!* now says softly, All this is not really happening.

'Oh no? Tell that to my foot and my chest!'

She orders herself to move, but her body does not want to know her. She is shaking with pain. Move! How? On hands and knees!

'They tell you to do this in the camps,' she remembers. 'And if you don't, they pull you along. To the shower rooms. They order you to take off your clothes. Throw your shoes on the pile. Nice showers after a long journey. Not me!' Move!

Her chest screams with pain. 'How far can you get like this? You won't even reach the corner, and they'll find you in the morning. You'll be the first person that they put on the lorry.'

Now Elise's arms and hands, and her good leg, are working for her. She has moved on to dry ground. She wants to get far away from the window. She will have to live with the pain. This will not kill her, not yet. But she cannot look again at the children's faces. They trusted her.

She is moving faster now. Suddenly she thinks, 'Did Eloise tell the Germans about their hiding place?' And then, 'Will Sabina, Stefan and the children think *I* told the Germans?' She begins to cry. 'No, no!' She is talking to Eloise now. 'I won't believe it. You're honest and good, I know it. Different, yes, but good.'

At last Elise gets round the corner. There is a soft wind here, coming off the hills. 'I need something to walk with,' she thinks. She looks around her. The moon is out, and the stars. It is a beautiful night. Too beautiful for all this.

She sees something against the wall in front of her. It is a large fork. Elise uses it to help her walk. In front of her and up the hill are trees and rocks that she can hide in. From the top of the hill there will be a wonderful view over the river. But the children will never see it. And the river will not stop moving. It knows nothing of people's happiness or pain.

Elise continues, taking small steps. The fork is a good 'leg', but it doesn't like hills.

'What will I tell Dad? He'll have to take me to hospital. Well here's a story for your notebook, Dad. I'll have to stay in the house. Carol won't like that. She'll have to stop painting and feed me with hot soup. But then I won't have to be silent all the time. And you – wait! You *are* crazy! This isn't Stephen country. It's Stefan country. It's 5 April 1944. Or, no – this pain! – it's 6 April.'

She remembers the other Stefan. The mysterious boy on the church steps. 'Why was he afraid of me? Now I know!'

'I need a place to lie down. I must sleep – rest.' Elise falls over a stone. The fork catches behind her good leg and she falls . . . She is too tired to protect herself. She falls on to soft earth.

Chapter 7   The Lorries

Elise wakes up and the pain is the same. It is early morning and there is a pale sun in the sky.

'I can't get away from here,' she thinks. 'Dad will miss me. And he did tell me: In this beautiful countryside, there are murderers . . . That's truer than you realize, Dad. And what will Carol think? Wasn't she cold towards me? Didn't she want me to live with my Mum? Perhaps people are looking for me already. Oh please find me before it's too late!'

She checks her state of health. She has slept on her left side. Her chest hurts. She tries to move, but then her head hurts. She exercises her neck.

'I can do it,' she tells herself. 'I've got to.' She smells the fresh grass. It gives her hope. And from somewhere above her she hears the birds singing. 'I've got to get away. But where to?'

She is not safe – she is too near the farm. She reaches for the fork. 'I must get into the trees, and lie down.'

Suddenly there are sounds from the village. The sounds of lorries!

Elise pulls herself towards a low wall of rock.

The lorries are leaving the road now and stopping in the yard. Soldiers jump out of the back. An officer steps down from the front of one. He shouts orders. The Gestapo have finished their work at Belley. Now it is the turn of Izieu.

Elise forgets the pain in her foot and chest. She stands up now. The yard is full of soldiers, holding guns.

Sabina? There is no Sabina. Was no one on guard last night? What happened to the careful eyes of Cerberus?

At the far end of the building, a ground-floor window has opened. Someone drops into the shadows at the side of the yard. One will escape. To tell the story.

The children are brought down. Some of them are only half-dressed. There are adults with them too. They are ordered into the lorries. Elise can see their faces: serious, pale and tired. No questions, no tears. The gates of the lorries are shut and locked.

The officer is giving an order to someone that Elise cannot see. He speaks in French.

Eloise understands: 'We will stop in the village. We will show the children to the village people. Then they will understand that the Gestapo knows everything. If anyone protests, shoot them.'

As quickly as they came, the lorries leave. There are no children now at the farm of Lolinoz. But one got away. Was it Stefan?

Inside her head, Elise talks to the children. 'Someone told the Germans about you . . .'

♦

Strange, but the foot doesn't hurt now. There is only an ache, like the ache in her heart. 'I must hurry,' she says to herself. 'Dad likes us all to sit together at lunch.'

But not this way, not past the farm. No. The path above her goes up and down between white rocks. It goes into the village from behind the church.

Poor Sabina. She will return this evening, walking up the road as usual. Will the farmer tell her? Or will he be too afraid to look at her?

'It was the girl!' Is that what they will say? 'People saw her in the village. She probably picked up a phone. Who told the Gestapo? How will we ever know? Eloise – she was trouble. And she wasn't Jewish, remember.'

As she climbs the hill above the valley, Elise looks back at the farm. There is no sign that there were children there. But Elise will tell the story of the children of Lolinoz; the ghosts of Izieu.

Chapter 8   Memories

'What happened to you? What's wrong with your foot?'

It was Carol's voice. Carol with her painting things in front of her. And the beginnings of a picture of the river, the trees and the rocks.

'So I wasn't missed,' thought Elise. 'The time is the time when I left. Nothing has happened. But *everything* has happened. It did happen. Things only *seem* to be the same.'

'I just fell, that's all.'

Carol's work for the morning was finished. She was happier now. 'Isn't it beautiful here? So quiet.'

'What date is it?' asked Elise.

She was always cold with Carol, so her stepmother was not surprised. Elise tried again, more softly: 'I'm sorry.'

'That's OK,' said Carol. 'I understand.'

'Do you?'

'We really must learn to be friends, Elise.'

'Today I was called Eloise,' said Elise.

Carol looked at her strangely. 'Are you all right?'

They were walking together down a dusty path towards the church. Without thinking about it, Elise put her hand around Carol's arm. This *was* a surprise; to both of them.

More kindly now, Elise asked again, 'What date is it, Carol?' She used her stepmother's name for the first time.

Carol noticed and smiled. To Elise, she seemed different, almost another person.

'Well yesterday was 5 April,' said Carol. 'So today ... Oh, there's your Dad by the church. I'll go and heat the soup. Bring him in five minutes, OK?'

'Thanks, Carol,' said Elise.

'For what?'

'You know – for trying.' Elise's thoughts returned to the farmhouse and her angry talk with Stefan. 'And I've said terrible things.'

Carol put an arm round her stepdaughter and gave her a kiss; their first kiss. 'We mustn't stop trying, must we?'

♦

'You knew about this place before we came, Dad. Am I right?' asked Elise. She put her arm through his, too.

'I want you to read this,' said Dad. There was writing on the metal plate of the war memorial. Below it were some fresh flowers. 'Can you understand the French, Elise?'

'This morning I met a boy called Stefan,' said Elise. 'He told me everything.'

Her father read out the story of forty-four children taken from their hiding place in the village. Taken by the Gestapo. There were tears in his eyes.

There was writing on the metal plate of the war memorial. Below it were some fresh flowers.

'They were never seen again,' he said. He looked at the spring flowers. 'All this time, but somebody remembers, Elise.' He stopped, but then continued. 'Where were you taken, little children? Dachau, probably. Did I ever tell you, Elise –'

'About the trains, Dad?' Elise said. The trains, yes. She remembered the children's 'train' in the farmhouse.

'We are going on a train?'

'Where to?'

'I love trains.'

'Will it be safe?'

'What does Madame Sabina say?'

'Terrible,' said Dad. 'The deaths. I just can't forget.'

To herself, Elise said, 'You're not the only one who can't forget.'

As they walked back to their holiday home, somebody was watching Elise from the steps of the church. She turned. For a second, the entrance to the church was the inside of a Gestapo lorry. The children were climbing in. No questions, no tears. The lorries moved away – to the trains. One person was left in the shadows of the church. He lifted a hand and waved to her.

'Have you hurt your foot, my pet?' asked Dad, noticing.

Elise fought back her tears. 'Yes, I ... Dad, can *we* put down some flowers, next to the others? Wild flowers, from up on the hill?'

'Why not?' Dad put his arm round his daughter. 'Things are going to get better now, I promise.'

'I know,' answered Elise. 'But Dad?' Her thoughts were with the ghosts of Izieu, her friends for ever. 'Flowers will never be enough.'

ACTIVITIES

Chapters 1–2

Before you read

1 Look at the pictures in the book. What do you think the story is about? Read the Introduction. Were you right?

2 Answer the questions. Find the words in *italics* in your dictionary. They are all in the story.

    a Who fights for an *army*?

    b Where in a bedroom do you find *curtains*?

    c If your room is *dusty*, what do you do?

    d Do you believe in *ghosts*?

    e Is a *grave* for a living person or a dead one?

    f Where can you see your *image*?

    g What are war *memorials* usually made of?

    h Who is married to your *stepmother*?

    i Who works in a *town hall*?

After you read

3 Answer these questions.

    a When did Elise's mother leave her father?

    b What does Elise see in the 'image'?

    c Where does Stefan live and work?

4 Who says these words? Who are they talking to?

    a 'You're new in our lives, and she's not sure about you.'

    b 'Why do you always visit those war graves?'

    c 'Don't look so worried. Nobody's going to hurt you.'

    d 'Your mother, she is the painter?'

Chapters 3–5

Before you read

5 Will Elise see Stefan again? Where? What do you think?

6 Make one or two sentences with each pair of words. Find the words in your dictionary.

   a *concentration camp   refugee*

   b *haunt   yard*

   c *arrest   risk*

   d *God   trust*

After you read

7 Finish these sentences.

   a Nobody has signed their name in the church Visitors' Book since . . .

   b The woman calls Elise by the new name of . . .

   c The woman takes Elise to . . .

8 How do these people feel?

   a Sabina about Eloise/Elise

   b Stefan about Eloise

9 Why did Stefan's parents have to wear yellow stars on their coats?

10 Work with another student. Act out this conversation.

   Student A: You are with the Gestapo. You want to know if any Jews are hiding in the area.

   Student B: You are a villager. You know that there are children near the village. You do not want to tell the Gestapo. But you have a family and you do not want to risk their lives.

Chapters 6–8

Before you read

11 What do you think will happen to the children at the farm? What will happen to Elise?

12 Find these words in your dictionary.

   march   protest   solution

   a What do people do on a protest march?

   b What is the 'final solution'?

After you read

13 Choose the best question-word for these questions, and answer them.

Why   What   How

   a ... happened when Elise's father went on protest marches?

   b ... does Elise wait by the window?

   c ... does Elise hurt her foot?

   d ... does Elise use to help her walk?

14 Find and correct the mistakes in these sentences.

   a Three lorries come into the farmyard with the German police.

   b Someone escapes from the Germans through an upstairs window.

   c The story of the children is in a book in the church.

Writing

15 Why does Elise's father visit war memorials? Do you agree with his opinions?

16 At the end of the story, Elise says, 'Flowers will never be enough.' What does she mean? Do you agree with her?

17 You have a time machine and can travel back to a time in the past. Which time would you like to visit? Why?

18 Did you enjoy this story? Why (not)? Think of another possible title for the story.

Answers for the Activities in this book are published in our free resource packs for teachers, the Penguin Readers Factsheets, or available on a separate sheet. Please write to your local Pearson Education office or to: Marketing Department, Penguin Longman Publishing, 80 Strand, London WC2R 0RL